Made in United States
Troutdale, OR
08/28/2023

12438504R00069